I0750264

FINISHING LINE PRESS
www.finishinglinepress.com

what mothers withhold

poems by

Elizabeth Kropf

Finishing Line Press
Georgetown, Kentucky

what mothers withhold

ISBN 978-1-64662-393-8 First Edition

ACKNOWLEDGMENTS

"what mothers withhold," © 2017 *di-verse-city* 2017, Anthology of the Austin International Poetry Festival
"what I wish to withhold" originally published as "poison" © 2014 *Blue Hole*
"upon the birth of my daughter" © 2011 *Ardent*
"heel-click" © 2013 Texas *Poetry Calendar*
"her alone;" "Austin bombs: March, 2018" ©2018 *Mothering with Imagination*, May/June 2018 edition

Publisher: Leah Huete de Maines
Editor: Christen Kincaid
Cover Art: Tamryn Spruill
Author Photo: Alejandra Alumbaugh Photography
Cover Design: Elizabeth Maines McCleavy

Order online: www.finishinglinepress.com
also available on amazon.com

Author inquiries and mail orders:
Finishing Line Press
PO Box 1626
Georgetown, Kentucky 40324
USA

Table of Contents

To: my children and almost children
and in memory of Devorah Winegarten

chocolate chip cookies with Madeline L'Engle

I wish for chocolate chips cookies, warm. I wish to dip them in milk.
Cow's milk- because there is no lactose intolerance in dreams

I wish to share them with Madeline L'Engle

I wish to scrape away the groves of disappointment that have crept
into my eight-year-old daughter's world

I wish to, with a small scalpel, carefully scrape away the plaque on the
brains of Alzheimer's patients

I wish to scrape away shame

I wish to scrape away PTSD: startled response, recurring nightmares
no medication can touch, memories breaking through mundane
moments

I wish to, with a warm wet washcloth, scrape away dirt from the feet
of the children walking to the United States from Honduras

I wish to give them milk, cookies, blankets around their shoulders as
they listen to Madeline L'Engle, who will whisper to them planets and
dolphins and all the forces aligned to keep them safe

ultrasound

tiny
waving arms, legs
unborn. I drown in fear
in love so fierce, all consuming
I break

the cost of obedience

naked in a paper gown
I am without a voice
I nod and accept. I do not say no.
Nurses stare at monitors, their backs to me.

Hours, hours.

A nurse starts an often delivered speech:
"you don't have to be superwoman."
Then, an epidural given without sympathy or precision.
I am as vulnerable as if I have no skin.

after
two doctors stitch me, discuss music.
I ask repeatedly,
when can I eat, when can I eat?
They say, *not yet.*

I obey, my body weak from a twelve hour fast.
I obey. Holding my breath, grasping for self
suspended in terror

until I go home two days later
cut the hospital tags
untethered, unmolested,

free to put myself together again.

upon the birth of my daughter

where was I in these moments
when they pulled you from my body

the pain, the instruments
a room of white coats
prepared for catastrophe
not mother meeting child

in this
I could not hear your first cry
let me reclaim this unmatched sound

I do not remember my first thoughts,
only your brown hair curly from the liquid of birth
your forehead swollen, expression alert

let me reclaim the first moment I held you,
handing you back so soon, arms too weak
let me reclaim, reclaim this passage
let me reclaim a tender moment
to remember, to tell you again and again

let me reclaim a place to give you birth
sacred and still
father, mother, child

let me reclaim each moment torn from me
torn from you

unraveling

It is the choice to postpone dreams we may never be able to claim.
A car spinning toward the center divider. So many spools,
so many words we yearn to unravel.
knotted, frayed threads kept out of sight.
These untidy, unbreakable threads: straightjacket or adornment.
If only it was simply the needle that pricked. Only in fairy tales
spun,

spun,
told for us to claim
our rights of adornment,
to collect these spools,
these secrets. As if we only needed to sew well, keep the prize in sight
so that we will not unravel

unravel.
we cannot cut these threads tangled around our fingers, spun
so tight. The children we loved without sight
of them. How could we know love was not enough to stake a claim
to keep them safe. That these spools
cannot spin our will, cannot guarantee adornment.

The patterns we choose, our preference of adornment,
we only hope it does not unravel.
We measure our spools
our tasks, our choices: spun.
Yet we can claim
so little. We try to keep composure in sight,

disappointment piling like inept metaphors. No clarity in sight.
Adornment,
a loosely woven prize to claim
it cannot always keep us warm. We can only hope it does not unravel
the lives we have spun.
The spools,

we gather the spools.
We clutch, always in sight,
how our lives have been spun.
Is it enough to cling to the adornment
of loved ones? Will it be enough when we unravel,
when we can no longer claim

friendships by trading baby showers. When adornment spools,
winds around the fabric and does not unravel, when our sight
adjusts, when we claim nothing—freedom is spun.

heel-click

our daughter's voice rises and falls with delight:
wordless vocabulary
our pit-bull, so gentle, endures hard pats and tugs

layers of dust, paper, laundry untouched
everything eclipsed by her seven-toothed grin

what mothers withhold

my four-year-old says she does not like when Elsa is mean to her sister
I try to explain that she is only trying to protect her

as I protect her with a sanitized, joyful version of her birth
as my mother protected me
leaving out for so long life-threatening hemorrhaging

as mothers have always withheld splinters of pain
unwilling to prick innocent skin
until the moment the child is ready to hold truth tenderly
accept blood trickle from sharp edges
until the child has eyes to see translucent change from shard to jewel
glistening with amniotic fluid, with the deepest shade of ruby,
with the shine of unbreakable diamonds

stir

"All the women whose heart stirred with a skill spun
the goat's hair." Exodus 35:26

We weave for the tabernacle, we emanate skill.
We groan,
endure for pregnancy.
Blood spun
into fabric of womb. Or, womb torn in miscarriage.
Yet, for love, for child, for God we stir.

Rahab know to hide God's men. Enemies did not stir
stalks on the roof. Deceit, the skill
of ages. Esther arranging miscarriage
of genocide- groan
of burial wraps spun.
Like so much pouring of body into self: pregnancy.

Before C-sections, birth control pills. The gamble of pregnancy.
What word did you have for umbilical cord? We stir
our children to greatness. Webs of wonder spun.
Men leave or stay. We break. Learn the skill
of putting ourselves together again. We groan
like the Holy Spirit, grief that cannot be uttered: miscarriage.

We crumble or resurrect, learn to whisper *miscarriage*
Leah was given pregnancy
without love. Each groan
unanswered. Still.
To love without reciprocity. A skill
mastered. Crimson threads spun.

Will we ever hear stories spun
lullabies Moses' mother sang, then, the dirge: miscarriage
of hopes floating down a river. Then, the skill
that brought Moses back to her breast, unexpected pregnancy
of dreams as if her son was born to her again. How did her heart stir,
and groan

with the weight of recovered joy? Or was that his groan
at lacking milk supply, his infant world spun
by the mother-switch. And how did Mary's mind stir
when she discovered her fate: miscarriage
of normalcy? A most unplanned pregnancy.
Did she weave His swaddling clothes; did her heart stir with a skill?

We weave the world, each other's miscarriages. With silence or groan,
with or without pregnancy, our lives are spun.
With skills of ages; of weaving, of carrying, of nursing, our hearts stir.

the tearing

with thanks to David Meischen

it is as if my daughter said
you are not enough, you must give more
my husband coughs
my mother puts a cold washcloth on my forehead
feeling the weight of what her own mother did not do
was not asked to do

doctor's hands reach inside to pull my daughter out
your body is not enough

it was the year of the earthquake in Haiti

how could I know then?
the tearing was to make room for the seven pound eight ounce weight
tearing to stretch skin
that I will bleed less
when she tears against my hand-stitched heart to break free

what a nanny withholds

Don't leave, Grace mouths from dance class. I'm held hostage
to the windows she can see me from. A triangle of anxiety:
I go find her twin Anna. She cries when she can't see me. Yet, time
has downgraded me to babysitter. I witness their independence:
the assertion that if we kill bees there'll be no more flowers. Always
I panic

at new phrases: "Who says we have to?" and "What the…?" They panic
if the routine of our goodbye is altered. I am hostage
to the last hug and kiss at the door. "You'll always
pick us up from school." First grade. Anxiety
over new things has not lessened. Their independence
arrives in spurts: Grace will be a pastry chef, Anna, a ballerina. Time

brought curiosity: what is my last name? They learn to tell time.
I panic
at questions about years from now: birthdays, gifts. My independence,
my dreams are suspended, held hostage
by the anxiety
of my absence from them. Always

I'll be held to the promise of scrapbooks on Christmas. Always,
until they outgrow me. In time
will one's anxiety
on the first day of school, the other's panic
over vaccinations lessen? I pray for them to be no longer held hostage
I want for my girls the independence

to keep them from sorrow over my inevitable leaving. The independence
to soothe themselves. The inevitability of leaving: always
holding me hostage.
Snapshots: Triumph over spelling a new word. The time
you thought you could swap identity, even being fraternal. Panic
when an E.R. visit separated you at bedtime. Anxiety

that the magician will make you disappear. My anxiety
that I reassure too much. That I offer too much independence-
the distance my girls can walk ahead of me. I panic
if they are not within sight. Have women always
held this fear so tight? All this time,
their sweetness, their flailing unselfconscious love holds me hostage.

Won't we always be this triangle trying to calm each other's anxiety?
Will time bring them independence
hostage only to love, never panic?

what I wish to withhold

guilt: a poison I am quick to drink
serve in long-stemmed wine glasses to others

how do I learn to detect this noxious odor
before swallowing without examination

how can I serve truth instead of guilt
and will it bring repentance?

how do I teach my young daughter the power of this poison?

sip when needed:

the singeing throat burn of wronging a friend
acid in the stomach propelling apology

how do I teach her
to guard what is placed in her cup
and by whom
to weigh what she pours out to others

that her hands may be clean
that her mouth taste her portion only

how not to get pregnant

Go off the pill.
Track your cycles,
symptoms and every substance
going in and out of your body.
Before getting out of bed,
take your temperature.
Do so without waking the child
next to you. Find a way to
remember your temperature until you find
a pen. Don't argue when you are ovulating.

Have sex regardless of mood.

Agonize
over whether to use vacation
days for sex or maternity leave.
Lie down for 15 minutes after sex to allow sperm to reach egg.
Cry if needed.
Overanalyze
every symptom
as your cycle ends.
Do not take a pregnancy test
until you are   late.

When your period
hits, have a bottle of wine
ready. Decide to stop trying.
Change your mind the next day.

Repeat.

a brief history of pelvic exams

1. instrument probes

    she tightens, digs heels in stirrups

2. fingers measure dilation

    she says I'm sorry

3. ultrasound searches for miscarriage remains

    she says *stop*, gets blood drawn instead

4. ultrasound searches for infertility cause. Invasive X-ray is ordered her body says *stop* her body says *no* her body says *enough*

confirmation

even squinting, there is no speck of life
artificial hope vanishes in the skirt-shaped window of the ultrasound
three stripes indicating future fertility, confirming the miscarriage is complete

her alone

October will not bring
siblings with perfect three year spacing

is it possible this death—
this time returned to us—is a gift,
an orb of healing: our daughter's first visit to the ocean
her first train ride
our arms for her alone

my milk,
my body, nourishing her alone
her breathing slowed in milk-drunk stillness
her babyhood extending like her arm across my chest

is it possible we don't know best what our family is supposed to be
who or what will fill this longing
as we open our hands
praying to endure what is placed there

at ten, the tangles in my hair so tight, I could not comb them

I had to get a boy's haircut
the shame of being mistaken for a boy, an eruption
why didn't my parents comb my hair?

the boy who tried to choke me without consequence
why didn't my parents act?

I piece together diagnoses that came later
wonder what lava-laden sorrows ignite in my daughters
as I place the oxygen mask over my own mouth?

Austin bombs: March 2018

we had to tell her not to open any packages

it was not the school shooting, not the church shooting, but bombs
that broke the perfect cloud of our seven-year old's innocence
so many tragedies she is unaware of

we had to tell her not to open any packages
we had to tell her

we read a children's book that uses the phrase *banana bombs*
a string of silly things starting with the letter *B*
she said "I have a connection. That is just like the bombs that went off"

first rip in a veil that will continue to tear
as tragedies are harder to conceal
what will remain of her tender spirit when the last realms of protection are removed
how can we save her?

"I am a promise. I promise to help of all the rabbits"

She bows, then steps back in line.
Whose idea was it
to dress a five year old in a cap and gown,
hand her a certificate for graduating preschool?
In the chaos of the ceremony, cap and gown are tossed aside before I get a picture
she takes the year 2016 off the tassel before we get home.
I blink, and it is 2028

I am again holding gifts she tosses aside
again the one saying goodbye to teachers
while she runs off to meet up with friends
bangs still in her eyes, still wearing long sleeves in May
leopard print boots peeking out from graduation gown

six-week ultrasound

"so you're here to see if this pregnancy is viable," the medical student says

after an almost undocumented pregnancy, lost too early for ultrasound,
this:
this barely perceptible fetus
measuring correctly
heart beating.
Heart beating.
Surely it will not stop.

self-weaning

she did not draw a poem from me until she drew blood
jaw clinching breast
swiftly, violently cutting me off
malicious, full-toothed grin
running away
her stance wide, sturdy
her legs strong

Elizabeth Kropf earned her Master of Arts in Creative Writing from Perelandra College and was honored to learn from writers Ken Kuhlken and Gary Swaim. Kropf has had over twenty poems in publications including *The Texas Poetry Calendar*, the *DEFY!* Anthology by Robocup Press, and several editions of *di-verse-city,* the anthology of the Austin International Poetry Festival. She has won awards from the Austin Poetry Society and Poetry Society of Texas.

After moving to Austin with her husband in 2001, she was fortunate enough to join the welcoming poetry community where she was encouraged to continue writing, notably from the late Devorah Winegarten. She attends local poetry festivals, poetry readings at BookWoman, and has hosted a critique group for over ten years.

The poems in *what mothers withhold* were written over a span of over ten years, bookending the birth and babyhood of her delightful daughters. Kropf's next book might be about fruit, pavement, or volcanoes. She is currently working on an ekphrastic poetry collaboration with artist Tamryn Spruill, who created the cover art for *what mothers withhold.*

www.ingramcontent.com/pod-product-compliance
Lightning Source LLC
LaVergne TN
LVHW051023080826
845145LV00009B/2775

* 9 7 8 1 6 4 6 6 2 3 9 3 8 *